distractions

distractions

Poems by
Miller Williams

Louisiana State University Press
Baton Rouge and London 1981

Designer: Patricia Douglas Crowder
Typeface: VIP Trump
Typesetter: G & S Typesetters, Inc.
Printer: Thomson-Shore, Inc.
Binder: John Dekker & Sons, Inc.

LIBRARY OF CONGRESS CATALOGING IN PUBLICATION DATA
Williams, Miller.
    Distractions.

    I. Title.
PS3545.I53352D5   811′.54   80-39502
ISBN 0-8071-0796-4
ISBN 0-8071-0797-2 (pbk.)

Thanks are offered to the editors of the following magazines, in which
some of the poems in this volume previously appeared, some in
different versions: *Barataria Review, Bits, Chariton Review, Cimarron
Review, Kayak, New England Review, New Orleans Review, Paint-
brush, Poetry, Poetry Miscellany, Poetry Northwest, Red Weather,
Shenandoah, Southern Review.*
Grateful acknowledgment is also made for permission to reprint and
translate the following: "Proverbios y Cantares," by Antonio Machado,
all rights reserved, the estate of Antonio Machado; "Muertes," by Pedro
Salinas, © Jaime Salinas and Soledad Salinas de Marichal; "Les
Primeurs," by Lucienne Desnoues, granted by the author; "Per
Pasolini," by Franco Fortini, granted by Arnoldo Mondadori Publishers;
"Herbsttag," by Rainer Maria Rilke, translated by Miller Williams in
Paintbrush. Reprinted by permission of New Directions Publishing
Corporation, publishers of Rainer Maria Rilke, *Selected Works.*

for Jordan

Contents

I know who you are and you don't;
You know who I am and I don't.

Tom T. Hall

I

Main Street

We came here to live in a small town.
Already the bypass half-encircles us,
the three-story houses on Maple Street are gone
except for one which is a funeral home
with sad blue blinking letters over the porch.

The streets are guarded by two-headed parking meters
which doesn't matter since half the stores closed down
after Sears and Penney's moved to the mall.

Now something neither town nor city takes over.
The hospital adds a wing. The census swells.
The city limits signs of six towns
move toward each other like suspicious children.

Our children whom we meant to raise as hicks
come strangely into the house and bring new words.
They are well-bred and come from good stock.
They join us always for breakfast. We see in their eyes
and in their smiles they are patient and willing to wait.

Love and How It Becomes Important in Our Day to Day Lives

The man who tells you which is the whiter wash,
the woman who talks about her paper towels,
the woman whose coffee holds her home together,
the man who smells the air in his neighbor's house,

the man who sings a song about his socks,
the woman who tells how well her napkin fits,
the man who sells the four-way slicer-dicer,
the woman who crosses tape between her tits,

and scores besides trample my yard, a mob
demanding to be let in, like Sodomites
yelling to get at my guests but I have no guests.
I crawl across the floor and cut the lights.

"We know you're there," they say. "Open the door."
"Who are you?" I say. "What do you want with me?"
"What does it matter?" they say. "You'll let us in.
Everyone lets us in. You'll see. You'll see."

The chest against the door begins to give.
I settle against a wall. A window breaks.
I cradle a gun in the crook of my elbow.
I hear the porch collapse. The whole house shakes.

Then comes my wife as if to wake me up,
a box of ammunition in her arms.
She settles herself against the wall beside me.
"The towns are gone," she says. "They're taking the
    farms."

There is an Amazon tribe that kills its children.

This tribe was only recently discovered.
Two hundred fifty are dead by white diseases.
They have decided to die by their own doing.

Every infant is blessed and fed and killed.
Summarily executed (this is Reuters).

They will be gone before the highway gets there
but there will be guides to explain it and you can drive
    by.

The Year They Outlawed Baseball

The year they outlawed baseball
nobody played.
The next year people said
how it used to be,
the centerfielder leaping up the wall.
The next year a few men tossed a few
in backyards and basements
without the gloves.
The ball gives off a sound
hitting the leather
anyone around could recognize.
Still people talked
and that was the end of that.
For years the widows kept scarred and lopsided balls
on the top shelves of closets in back rooms
and thought of showing them to trusted friends.

Sometimes You Stand There
Waiting for the Paper To Be Delivered

Late January.
Snow is on everything.
No matter how far I listen there is only silence.

Two yellow machines have worked for a week
cutting away the hill in front of the house
I have come to live in for the rest of my life.

On the highest part of the hill
one oak is standing.

Nothing else is vertical on the horizon.
It locks the white sky to the white earth.

The Art of the Practical

Not patriotism nor love of contesting gods
nor thirst for glory nor fears nor fortitudes
nor hate of iniquity but dollars and cents
make senators and wars and such other events.

A Good Woman

When the sails are furled all winds are the same.
Clement Long

9

He did or didn't whatever he did or meant to
and came and went.
She made the coffee strong and stacked the plates,
took off her clothes and said she thought so too.

But then it came to pass:
"Well," she said.
"Well," he answered. "Well. Alas. Alack."
She kissed him on the head and shook his hand.
"All's well that ends," she said, and never came back.

You have to think of Eve.
You have to think of Lot's wife and Sarah.
Bluebeard's women. Antigone. Pandora.
It was always the women who pissed the gods off,
        pushing,
never able to leave things alone.
That was when gods were gods, and they laid them low.

The children are grown and gone. A good thing.
They say she's taken up with someone else.
Nobody we know.

The News

When we saw the guerrilla get shot in the head
his face flattened as if a fist had hit it.
He collapsed like clothes left standing empty
by a street magician suddenly disappeared.

I saw a woman once come out of her window
and fall with a flower pot for twenty floors,
her panties horribly public. Her long fingers.

And houses floating and people sliding off.
School books and jackets scattered half a mile.
Trains turned over and turtles laying eggs.
Most every day I see the president.
And all those people in pain, dying in pain,
or facing the camera saying, "I beg your pardon."
A woman jumping at last. Goodbye. Goodbye.

I also have my books and good music.
I have a bottle of cold white wine.

My grandfather saw in all his eighty years
one gunfighter go down in a street in Kansas.

I understand the difference in death and art.
I understand the woman out of the window
was giving all she had in a hard performance
so far as I could see from curtain to curtain;
those who watched her go in the good flesh
have seen plain death and some will dream about it.
Art is not life, but what it is it is.
We've seen figures run across the moon,
hostages released and mad kings.

He told me he could smell the gunpowder still.
He said the man was lifted off the ground.

He was eighty-three years old when he told me this.

II

The Well-Ordered Life

Once he went inside a pool hall.
The clicking billiard balls put him in mind
of African tribes who click to say, "I love you"
"What do you want?" "We're going to kill you, of
    course."
They skirted the circles of light in a secret frenzy.

He took his Instamatic every week
and thirty-five dollars to life class.
He didn't use film. He couldn't have hidden the
    pictures.
He circled and focused and framed. The breast and knee.
The purest art he said is the briefest art.

Once he hunted for love. A long time
he stood beside a little fat lady,
dressed in red, standing on the corner,
looking something like a fire hydrant.
She boarded a bus and left him there alone.

Daily the desperate ordering of this world,
the objects on his desk, the chosen words,
the knife, fork and spoon, the folded napkin,
the one, two, three, the counting, counting,
a constant laying of sandbags on the levee.

The Chair

The man who talks with his fingertips together,
the woman who twists the buttons on her blouse,
are sitting in a room with an empty chair
making small and tentative observations
on politics and the weather. They are waiting
    for you to come and sit in the other chair.

They don't know how skillful you've become
at keeping that room out of your head,
that you've forgotten their names and don't know
you ever knew them. They believe you will come.

They look at the chair. They never mention it.
They ask themselves whatever could have happened,
why you take so long. But they believe,
they'd claim they have good reason to believe,
you're coming soon. He makes a sort of joke.
She shifts and glances toward the chair. She smiles.
Not what you would call a good smile.

Professor

He sits in the room alone, imagines a storm
torn in strips from all the remembered storms
out of The Odyssey, The Ancient Mariner, Oz.
Somewhere inside the storm, a grey room
collects itself out of the House of Usher,
out of Beowulf and Dover Beach.
Two people are making love in the room,
throwing on the wall the flowering shadows
of all the remembered lovers, the terrible
and gentle remembered lovers, Sons and Lovers,
Paradise Lost, Padua, that little book
somebody passed around in the tenth grade
showing couples out of the comic strips
leading a second life. He sees out the window
the long-legged women of spring, taking walks.
He rolls them over his tongue. He thinks of names.
Anna Karenina. Moll Flanders. Blondie.

The Survivor

According to the helicopter pilot,
the staticky talk on the two-way radio,
the next crest and the next
up a dry wash a mile or so
and there: the tail fin first, a wing, unusual odors.
No one seems to be alive but a woman,
standing there as still as the topless trees,
her left arm hanging loose in the crusted sleeve.

"What are your thoughts on being the sole survivor?"
says the reporter, stumbling beside the stretcher.

Says the lady, "Sir—," and then the stretcher slipping,
she slides free and falls a hundred feet,
tumbling down the mountain, loosening rocks.

Some would say the ribbon she has in her hair
fluttered loose when she fell and was found
almost at once
by a large bird, white, or more gray than white.
This is not so.

The Ones That Are Thrown Out

One has flippers. This one is like a seal.
One has gills. This one is like a fish.
One has webbed hands, is like a duck.
One has a little tail, is like a pig.
One is like a frog
with no dome at all above the eyes.

They call them bad babies.

They didn't mean to be bad
but who does.

He learns what love can do and what it can't do.
He sees it in her face more than he wants to.

He recognizes the interrogative touch
he can't decipher and doesn't like too much.

Sometimes they do lie down together
and feel at home in the grace of one another.

This is not what he thought it would be,
but nothing else is, either. She would agree.

The Home

The hand that pulls back the attic curtain,
the face that appears a moment in the window,
belongs to no one that you would have known
if you had lived here for fifty years.
If you had lived here for fifty-one
you would have known about the barber's daughter,
an ugly thing who swept her father's shop
and lacked a tongue, which finally she found
or so they say, in the Tenth Street Gospel Tent
where faithfully she was on Sunday mornings,
where only she and one young farmer went
Saturday nights until her father found them
going at it, using the name of God.
He made them kneel there naked so they say
and tore their flesh and took the tent to the ground.
Nobody here remembers when she came,
how come they let her keep the fruit jars.

There was a woman who was marked. Her mother
went when she was pregnant with this child
down to the slaughter pen to see her husband
kill a calf, it being the family pet.
When this child was born her hands and feet
were hooves. She never stood nor sat up.
Her tongue was large and rough. She couldn't talk.
She learned to read. Some days a woman came
to turn the pages. Also there was a hymn
How Tedious and Tasteless the Hours that she could
    hum.

Joe Deal who came from somewhere else
only cares about himself.
He was raised by ugly aunts
who poured molasses in his pants.

He laughs and rocks and sings their praise
through all the long and changeless days.
They get him where he goes to hide.
Come on they say It's time you died.
Go fuck he says and sings his song.
Everything I've done is wrong.
He goes to bed and masturbates
and hugs his skinny knees and waits.

Miss Olivia Bliss who wets her chair,
Whose breath is caught in heaves and lost in slumps,
has outlived all her sons and all her daughters
and even some of their daughters and sons are dead.
She has gone off and left her eyes, her ears.
She tests the air with her tongue. To tell from her face
it tastes as bad as it tasted yesterday.

Pick out some things and put them in a box,
objects to count, to take out and return:
a couple of shapes that feel good to the fingers:
a set of keys, a fountain pen, a watch;
one time at a kitchen window, a cup of coffee;
driving west at midnight, someone asleep.

Who is it sleeping there in the front seat?

Getting the Message

Hermes it was. Hermes with wingéd heels,
looking like an ad for FTD.
I woke to see his silhouetted frame
inside the window frame. Hermes it was.
With, I had to assume, a message for me.

He wore the same hard hat he always wore,
suggesting a nudist on a construction crew,
except the hat had wings. Except also,
he wasn't entirely nude. The ribbon flapped
and did precisely what it was meant to do.

Not meaning to seem a churl, a poor host,
nor wanting to seem too easily surprised
by this event, this hour of the morning
here in a Houston hotel, and thus appear
outside of myth and thus uncivilized,

and on the other hand, not wanting to seem
so gullible as to think the man was there
if it should turn out later he never was,
I lay in a shape that may have been described
if I were standing up as devil-may-care.

The hat's wings fluttered once. He shifted the hat.
"My name," he said, "is Hermes." "I know," I said.
I figured I could give him credence enough
for a civil response, at which response he entered
and scooted my feet aside and sat on the bed.

He asked if I was me. I said I was,
but I was not the one about whom doubt
might naturally arise and did he suppose
I'd be convinced as easily as that.
"Convincing you is not what I came about."

The tone was matter-of-fact. "I have a message."
"I take it you do," I said, "if you're in fact
an entity." "I have a message for you
whether I'm an entity or not.
There's no need for rudeness." "So how do I act

when Hermes comes in the window? Please understand
I'm trying to keep a fix on what we call
the phenomenological world. It isn't easy."
"That's what the message is about," he said.
"I'll have to have your promise, first of all,

not to tell anybody about the visit."
"What possible difference," I said, "could it make to you?
Nobody would believe it." "No difference," he said.
"It's like the apple, or never looking back.
There has to be something you're not allowed to do."

"How do you know I'll do what I say?" I said.
"When I tell about it—were I to—
I'd know already what the message is."
"So you would," he said. "But in that case,
whatever I tell you turns out not to be true."

He plucked a quill and pulled from under his hat
a packet of papers. "If you would please sign here."
I signed the promise. He rose in a flurry of wings.
The message, in a swirling cursive, read
What ought to happen happens in one year.

Mythic people like that sort of thing.
They tell you something that looks fine at first.
I've pondered it these past eleven months.
Now it's told, untold, there's nothing to tell.
Whatever it saved us from, or what it cost,
whether I lost us heaven, or spared us hell,
a die's uncast, a Rubicon uncrossed.

Ghosts

Some evenings, there are ghosts. There are. Ghosts
come in through the door when people come in,
being unable to open doors themselves
and not knowing (not knowing they are ghosts)

they could pass through anything, like thought.
They come and stand, move aimlessly about
as if each one of them had come to meet
someone who hadn't arrived. I always thought

of haunts and spirits as having a special power
like witches to do whatever they wanted to.
They don't. Pure energy without a cage
can do nothing at all. Whatever power

pushes or pulls the things of this world
to any purpose does it by piston or pistol,
mill wheel or spring or some such pushing back.
Spirit freed fades into the world.

Inertia, which is habit, holds their lines
a little while and then like memories
they weaken and fade. The glow is energy going.
They seem like actors trying to remember lines.

The trouble is they don't know they're dead.
We don't know very much about ghosts;
we think that some of those who aren't prepared
and die surprised don't understand they're dead.

They hang around. The kindest thing to do
when you see one is simply to say
"Listen, you're dead. You're dead. Get out of here."
That's what the ghost eventually will do

when we've told it again and again to go.
"Get out of here. Get out of here. You're dead."
They can't of course go anywhere on purpose;
you have to give them intent to make them go.

And who knows where? All this has to do
with Newton's laws. The figure disappears.
Somewhere there's a place. Be kind. Be firm.
Remember the only thing you have to do

is tell them the truth. Say "You're dead. Get out."
Ignore the slow confusion on their faces.
Never pity. They can soak up pity.
Sympathy makes them denser and drags it out.

If pity comes, don't let it go to them.
Watch for a sudden change in temperature.
You still have a death to deal with.
Pity yourself, who could be one of them

to live—as it were—with all the embarrassment.
You would not want someone who sounds like
a movie director telling you you're dead.
Your tissue hands could not hide the embarrassment.

On the Last Page of the Last Yellow Legal Pad
In Rome
Before Taking Off for Dacca on Air Bangladesh

Well, you go back then to the central question.
What if you saw, say, Augustus Caesar,
relaxing around a bus stop, reading a paper?
What if you knew that you were awake and sane?
What would you know more than you know already?

You would know that there was life after death.

Or maybe that death doesn't take. What else would you
    know?
You want to say you would know that God existed.

It would weigh the evidence in his favor.
What could you do with a soul but not a god.
You would assume they have to go together.

It doesn't make any difference what we assume.

Still there's logic though and natural law.

Logic lies and natural law accounts
for the fall to earth of every plane that's fallen.

We've reached the end of the back of the last page.
They're calling the flight.

                        We still have all the margins.

Give it up. We never had the margins.

Suppose you saw, say, Cicero or Catullus?

You've got your ticket. Go get on the plane.

I'm trying to tell you something.

                        I know. I know.

Late Show

Too tired to sleep I switch a picture on,
Turn down the sound to let my attention drain.
A forest in summer. Dogs. A man is running.
It's starting to rain.

The man comes to a house. He breaks a window.
A girl getting out of the shower admiring herself
looks to see if the cat has knocked something
from the kitchen shelf.

She sees the man. She wraps a towel about her.
In the woods loosed from their leashes the dogs
are running in circles scratching at empty trees
sniffing at logs.

The woman is breathing behind a chair in the kitchen.
The man is leaning against the kitchen door.
Her mouth moves. He hits her in the face.
She falls to the floor.

He tears the towel away. He stands above her.
He looks a long time. He lets her curl
into a corner. Both of us can see
she is only a girl.

He takes her to her bed and drops her in it.
Looks at her as if he has not seen her
before now. Takes off his clothes and puts
himself between her.

He moves his lips. She bends her legs and locks him.
They move together. I turn up the sound.
They stop moving. They look in my direction.
A single hound

is crouping close. She shoves the man aside,
rolls out of bed, runs with nothing around her
into the rain, into the leaping dogs.
Lightning and thunder.

He sits on the bed, his back a slow curve.
Turn it off, he says, in god's name.
The door opens. A man with a long gun.
He takes aim.

Ways to say goodbye are going with him.
Words he said to his woman when she died
were long since said for the last time.
The nurse bends down.
"Do you hear me?"

He gives her the twenty syllables of summer.
She will be the last person to hear them.
"The fever," she says.

Hello

I'll sit down sooner or later. Untying my shoes
I'll look up at the sky and say Hello, Sky.
Look, people will say, He's come to his senses.
I've said Hello to walls. Nobody has said
A man has come to his senses, come and look.
But sooner or later I'll take a drink and sit down
and look into blue space and say Hello, Space,
and people will whisper, He's come to his senses, look.

Trying To Remember

You know in the muddy pond the fish is there.
It bumps the bait and late in the long shadows
it nudges a brief circle over the surface.
Give it up. It will die in the dark water.

In Scene One Act Two the Blond Boy
Falling Into Step Beside You Says

These are the ways in which people can die:
on purpose, by accident, of illness, of old age.
Old age is divided further into lonely
or crowded with children grown and grandchildren.
Illness is either lingering or brief.
The accident is yours or someone else's
accident he turns to let you in on.
The purpose you die for
supposing you die on purpose
may be yours or may be anyone's;
this allows for suicides, heroics
and murders of all kinds,
by strangers on the street,
in bathrooms by lovers and sad wives.
Death itself doesn't have divisions,
so far as we know.
There are rumors, generally discounted.

God

32

If it weren't for the dog, I think it would be all right.
Not that it doesn't get old. It does get old.
Try to keep in mind at the same time
the constant green sedan that circles the block,
the quadriplegic tied to the wheelchair,
the head floating on nothing, the faith healer
calling his dry mother, forth, come forth,
yellow flowers on the windowsill,
the president bringing the liquor to his lips,
bending his head to help, his eyes aiming,
the boy and the woman all a Saturday morning,
twisting in the damp and happy sheets.
Call them by name, call each of them a name.
Love them, prepare to punish and love them all.
Does anybody know whose dog that is?

He knows how few people get to be
even if there seem to be a lot.
Every day he's pleased to be among them
but knows he wouldn't mind if he were not.

The Fall of Skylab

What do we say about it going down?
Do we point out the fall of men and eagles,
philosophers and armies? For godsake,
not Icarus.
No more of Icarus.

Hell, Icarus doesn't fit here anyway,
where it's not the sun
but the hard air of home that does you in.

Oh the winds of space are cold winds
and the dark of space is long,
space is pure and silent
but the strings of earth are strong.

What else is there to say? My son, my son,
it's better than staying out there forever.

The Proper Study

Looking In
    A man comes home. He finds the door of his house
    blocked by a blue anteater with seven heads,
    red coals for teats, a tail of mottled smoke.
    In the window he sees his aged mother
    rocking in her lap a pig he knows
    for that same pig who built a house of straw.
    Get out of my way he says to the middle head.
    Growl says the middle head Growl. The others
        smile
    the way we have all observed anteaters smiling
    in situations exactly like this.

Looking Out
    A man studies the heavens, the constellations,
    one of the constellations, stares at a star,
    says one day at the biggest telescope
    leaping about, putting his spectacles on,
    it's not a star, it's not a star, it's a hole!

Fifty

36 _____

Wait. What

has happened here?

For Rebecca, For Whom Nothing Has Been Written Page After Page

We have a language that serves us more or less
for the earth and air and fire and the earth's water,
that sort of thing, for hydrogen and tin.

What phrase explains, what simile can guess
a daughter's daughter? We half know who you are,
moment by moment, remembering what you were
as you grow past, becoming by quick revisions
an image in the door.

What matters when all the words are written and read
is what remains not said, not said,
which is what long silences are for.

All He Ever Wanted

A good friend, a casually chosen book,
a couple of perfectly rotten magazines,
hot bread, cold milk, lean sausage and one good cook
who knows precisely what over-medium means.

III

Think of how in a hurricane the winds
build up from nothing at all and suddenly stop
then start the opposite way and die down,
the way the traffic around a stadium
builds to the game, stops, starts again
going the other direction, dies down.
Think in the eye of a hurricane, then, of Tittle,
Thorpe and Namath, Simpson, such acts of God.
At a football game, think of the gulf coast,
Biloxi, Mississippi blown away.

Words

Strip to the waist and have a seat. The doctor
will be in soon. He smiles and the nurse smiles.
He sits on the table, bumping his knees together,
scratching around his navel, counting the tiles.

We never talk, she says, and so you talk
and everything you speak of falls apart.
This is how we come to understand
what they mean by chambers of the heart.

Some words are said to start a conversation.
Some, after which there's nothing more to say.
"Amen," for instance. "I said I was sorry."
"Tower, we're going down. This is PSA."

Style

Sometimes he would try to write a poem
and what he wanted to do was scribble circles
down one side of the page and up the other
and once he did but he knew it wasn't a poem
although there were those who would have called it one
assuming of course that it was done sincerely.

Not wanting to waste the paper or the time
and having a dean impressed by anything,
he titled it and signed it and sent it off
and there it was in the Golden Rule Review,
"Poem in Sincere Circles." It was sincere.
A few months later it got anthologized.

He sits at his desk devising variations,
starting in the center of the page,
circles in circles with small symbols in them.
He publishes everywhere and gets letters
asking for explanations he never gives.
Also he never gives readings anymore.

Believing

There is a myth
persisting among a few African tribes
and some inhabitants of the Greek Islands
that says a building will not last a year
unless the builder seals inside its walls
the head or heart or body
(depending on the land you hear it in)
of somebody dear
wife or child or friend
close enough for a sense of sacrifice.

Where could he be I've called and called
Have you seen him

Listen how's the building coming along
Fine how would you like to have a beer
at my place
Anyone from Africa will tell you
a chicken head
which shows you how a myth can wear away
is hidden in the mud of every hut.

But now and then you read
from France or Sweden
about the trial of a builder
of skyscrapers for murder unexplained
of a good friend
a wife or a child.

Sometimes still when buildings are torn down
we read of skeletons.

We always assume of course
falling into trouble
some casual tenant.

Believing in Symbols

1

One morning I put in the pocket of my shirt
not having put two and two together
a little calculator. That afternoon
it lay on my desk and turned out 8s for hours,
shorted through by those rippling shocks
the sinus node sends out, now beat, now beat.

So what do we say for science and the heart?
So with reason the heart will have its way?

Believing in symbols has led us into war,
if sometimes into bed with interesting people.

2

8 becomes in the time of solid state
the figure all the figures are made from,
the enabling number, the all-fathering 8;
1 through 7, also nothing and 9,
are all pieces of 8 which is only itself.

This makes a certain sense if you look at the sign
that says infinity, the Mobius strip,
a lazy 8 hung on the gates of Heaven.

The pterodactyl, Pompeii, the Packard;
things take their turns. 3 and 7 are only
numbers again. Nothing stays for long.
Not to say that physics will ever fail us
or plain love, either, for that matter.
Like the sides of a coin, they may take turns,
or flipping fast enough, may seem to merge.

Call it, if you call it, in the air.
When the coin comes down, the tent comes down.
You look around, and there is nothing there.
Not even the planets. Not even the names of the
     planets.

Lying

Standing beside a library in Brooklyn
I wait for my ride to come. I turn some pages.
A man puts his foot on a fire hydrant
and bends to tie his shoe. I see a gun.
He sees me see the gun. The look is to tell me
I think I'm going to blow your navel away.
Looking back I start to tell it right.
It happened in Santa Fe. A small room.
Say a neighbor who knows I took his wife.
His wife hiding naked behind the door.
Guerrillas kicking the door in. Come with us.
The sack over the head. A house of strangers.
They've made a mistake they tell me and laugh about it.
I have to find my own way home.

Pity and Fear

In westerns the man who saddles up at night
is not going to say goodbye to someone
pretending to be asleep in the still cabin.
Which is to say he loves her and didn't mean to.
All she knows about him are dusty lies.
He stopped here to give his horse some water.
Or so he said. He stopped. It doesn't matter.
The man who saddles up his horse knows something.
What about her man? Will he not know?

Oh he will know, though he will never say it.
He will know his wife is not his woman.
He will become the sheriff and be a good one.

We see a passing of years. The man returns.
A windy desert town he barely remembers.
The tall son of the sheriff is dark and quick.

He gambles some. The women like him. His name
is Larry or Jim. He has his mother's eyes.
We know what will happen. Still we sit. We wait.

About the Airplane, Then

Looking out the window, across the room,
I saw a plane heading toward the west.
I thought as I often do when I see a plane
of who might be on board and what they wish
they'd said before they left or not said,
those they love and those they meant to love.
The plane seemed so small at such a distance,
and seemed to move so slowly, it might have been
some little creature crawling across the screen.
It stopped as if to consider that a while,
changed directions slightly and crawled on.

Inside my head two hundred and seventy people
including a crew of eleven disappeared
leaving no trace but only vacancies
at typewriters, bedtime and breakfast. It came so fast
nobody had a hint of what was coming
except for one especially perceptive
flight attendant who seemed to be startled
about something just at the last moment.

The Woman in the Room

She stands at the foot of my bed and starts to speak,
pauses, looks confused and fades out,
the colors of pressed flowers, a sickly smell,
then nothing. A wide skirt once, a flowered blouse.
Pale naked once. The moon by daylight
has almost the color. The first time
she wore a blue gown. She had a rose
pinned to the waist, lace around her wrists.

Listen, Woman. Woman, I never loved you.
I'm not the man you remember. This may be the room.
The house has been here for generations.
If you could tell me what you're trying to say.

That's what I always say or something like it.
Or mean to. I don't say anything.
She opens her mouth and no sound comes out.
There isn't any air but the air she is.

Little by little I'm learning to read her lips.

Evening: A Studio in Rome

The window here is hung in the west wall.
It lays on the opposite wall a square of light.
Sliced by the lopsided slats of the broken blind,
the light hangs like a painting. Now, and now,
the shadow of a swallow shoots across it.

I turn around to see the birds themselves,
scores of birds, hundreds, a thousand swallows.
I try to keep a single bird. I lose it.
In all that spinning not one bird spins loose.

I turn away from the window and back to work.
My eyes are caught again by the square of light.
I lean back in my chair and watch the picture
moving up the wall, the single birds
living out their lives in a frame of light,
until it touches the ceiling and fades out.
I turn around again and the swallows are gone.
The sun is gone. This minute Rome is dark
as only Rome is dark, as if somebody
could go out reaching toward it, and find no Rome.

IV

Parallel Lines
Some poems in translation

Herbsttag

Herr: es ist Zeit. Der Sommer war sehr gross.
Leg deinen Schatten auf die Sonnenuhren,
und auf den Fluren lass die Winde los.

Befiehl den letzten Früchten voll zu sein;
gieb ihnen noch zwei südlichere Tage,
dränge sie zur Vollendung hin und jage
die letzte Süsse in den schweren Wein.

Wer jetzt kein Haus hat, baut sich keines mehr.
Wer jetzt allein ist, wird es lange bleiben,
wird wachen, lesen, lange Briefe schreiben
und wird in den Alleen hin und her
unruhig wandern, wenn die Blätter treiben.

RAINER MARIA RILKE

Autumn

Lord, it is time. The perfect summer is past.
Lay your shadow across the sundials.
Let loose your winds on the fields. Command the last

green fruits to fullness, tree, bush and vine;
give them another two southerly days.
Move them on to their perfection. Chase
the final sweetness into the heavy wine.

Who has no house now will have no house.
Who is alone will be alone, will wake,
will read, will write long letters, will take
evening by evening slow and aimless walks
where brown leaves swirl and small winds rise and
        break.

Les Primeurs

On va déballer la fraîcheur du monde,
Les fruits, les primeurs, les cageots de fleurs.
Matin maraîcher, bombe et te débonde,
Halles et marchés, hissez vos couleurs!
L'aube des cités regorge de feuilles,
On va désangler les cressons puissants.
Sur leur dos carré—hisse!—les accueillent
Les forts du carreau, les donneurs de sang.

Qui parle toujours d'aurores malades,
D'hommes écoeurés par le soleil neuf?
Voici sous leur faix de vertes salades
Les buveurs de blanc, les mangeurs de boeuf.
O printemps du jour, heures vivrières,
C'est bien décidé par tout l'univers:
On veut vivre encor la journée entière,
Et croquer du ferme, et mâcher du vert.

On veut trois repas et quatre services
Mais que la pitance ait l'esprit subtil.
On veut les jardins au fond du délice
Et dans les raviers la moelle d'avril.
On veut que midi resplendisse et chante
Tout enguirlandé d'orgueil végétal,
D'artichauts aigus coupés dans l'acanthe,
D'ail et de poivrons vernis au mistral.

Saint-Germain-des-Prés, si loin des prairies,
Voici le rachat des nuits de tabac,
Et qu'en plein poitrail du Paris qui crie
Le coeur délicat des Vaucluse bat
Ah! Voici la fleur des saisons pucelles,
Voici le tribut des champs jouvenceaux,
De l'asperge vierge à pleines nacelles
Et du radis rose encore au berceau.

First Things

We come to uncrate the newness of this world,
First fruits of the season, the crates of flowers,
Orchard morning, burst and lying open,
Markets, raise your colors. Dawn is ours.
Dawn in the cities, gorged with leaves; we come
To loose the bonds of the watercress. The men
Get braced to take it—eavoe!—across their backs,
Strong men, the givers of blood, they give it again.

These are not the men who hate the sun,
The ones that talk about the sick dawn;
These are men who stumble under salads
And eat the red meat and guzzle the wine.
Oh Spring of the day, the consecrated hours,
Now the whole universe agrees:
We still have time to live the day through,
To crack the hard bread, to chew the greens.

We ask for three meals, and only hope
For a little subtlety. It's a simple wish,
To find the gardens in the depths of pleasure,
The marrow of April deep in the first dish.
We want a sense of the south, resplendent and singing,
Growth like a proud green garland, thick skins
Of sharpened artichokes carved like acanthus,
Garlic, pepper polished in the winds.

Saint-Germain-des-Prés, so far from the fields,
Here's redemption for all the tobacco nights,
Here, set in the breast of clattery Paris,
Beats the simple proper heart of Provence.
Ah, the homage of the young fields,
Virgin asparagus barely out of the ground,
Flower of the virgin season; these radishes,
still lying in the cradle, pink and round.

Mon coeur débardeur, empoignons la vie.
Qui parle toujours d'aube à l'abandon?
Journée, ô laitue, enfant-de-Marie,
Que j'aime palper ton joli bedon.
Je happe à deux mains les seins de Pomone,
Son corset d'osier craquant de candeur.
Vigueur au quintal, tendresse à la tonne,
Etreignons-les dur, mon coeur débardeur!

Lucienne Desnoues

My stevedore heart, grab hold, grab hold of life.
Lettuce, Oh lettuce, all you poor green dummies,
Who can talk of a wasted dawn, daylight?
How I love to touch your lovely tummies!
In both my hands I hold Pomona's breasts,
Innocence pushing the wicker corset apart,
Strength in a kilo, tenderness in a ton,
Hold on hard, hold on, my stevedore heart.

Primero te olvidé en tu voz.
Si ahora hablases aqui,
a mi lado,
preguntaría yo: "¿Quien es?"

Luego, se me olvidó de ti tu paso.
Si una sombra se esquiva
entre el viento de carne,
ya no sé si eres tú.

Te deshojaste toda lentamente,
delante de un invierno: la sonrisa,
la mirada, el color del traje, el número
de los zapatos.

Te deshojaste aún mas:
se te cayó tu carne, tu cuerpo.
Y me quedó tu nombre, siete letras, de ti.
Y tú viviendo,
desesperadamente agonizante,
en ellas, con alma y cuerpo.

Tu esqueleto, sus trazos,
ut voz, tu risa, siete letras, ellas.
Y decirlas tu solo cuerpo ya.
Se me olvidó tu nombre.
Las siete letras andan desatadas;
no se conocen.
Pasan anuncios en tranvias; letras
se encienden en colores a la noche,
van en sobres diciendo
otros nombres.

Dying

First I forgot your voice.
If you should say something now,
here at my side,
I would say: "Who's there?"

Then I forgot your walk.
A shadow slips by
just brushing over my flesh
and I don't know if it's you.

Everything falls away slowly
before winter: the smile,
the gaze, the colors of your clothes,
the size of your shoe.

You keep falling away.
Your flesh, your body goes
and I'm left with your name, seven letters.
And you there alive
hopelessly dying
inside them, soul and body.

Your skeleton, its pattern,
your voice, your laugh, seven letters.
The pronouncing of them, your only body.
I forget your name.
The seven letters all disconnected
fly by unrecognized
on the sides of busses,
burn themselves neon in the night
travel on envelopes spelling
other names.

Por allí andarás tú,
disuelta ya, deshecha e imposible.
Andarás tú, tu nombre, que eras tú,
ascendido
hasta unos cielos tontos,
en una gloria abstracta de alfabeto.

PEDRO SALINAS

This is how you go on,
dissolved, undone, impossible
until finally you, your name, what used to be you
ascends
into some stupid heaven
some abstract alphabetical glory.

Nunca perseguí la gloria
ni dejar en la memoria
de los hombres mi canción;
yo amo los mundos sutíles,
ingrávidos y gentiles
como pompa de jabón.
Me gusta verlos pintarse
de sol y grana, volar
bajo el cielo azul, temblar
súbitamente y quebrarse.

*

Nuestras horas son minutos
cuando esperamos saber,
y siglos cuando sabemos
lo que se puede aprender.

*

Virtud es la alegría que alivia el corazón
más grave y desarruga el ceno de Caton.
El bueno es el que guarda, cual venta del camino,
para el sediento el agua, para el borracho el vino.

*

La envidia de la virtud
hizo a Caín criminal.
¡Gloria a Cain! Hoy el vicio
es lo que se envidia más.

*

No extrañéis, dulces amigos,
que esté mi frente arrugada;
yo vivo en paz con los hombres
y en guerra con mis entrañas.

*

I have never looked for glory,
my songs set in men's minds.
I prefer more subtle worlds,
the light and gentle kinds.
I like to watch a bubble take
the colors of the sun and hay,
rise, begin to float away, shake
suddenly and break.

                *

Hours are minutes dragging past
when we hope to know. They turn
to centuries when we come to know
all that we can ever learn.

                *

Virtue is what relieves the grave heart,
smooths the frown of the judge, lessens the fine.
The good is what protects, what opens the road:
for the thirsty water, for the drunkard wine.

                *

For envy of virtue Cain
forfeited paradise.
Glory be to Cain
We envy vice.

                *

Don't be concerned, dear friends,
at my wrinkled brow. These ruts
are from living at peace with my fellowmen
and at war with my guts.

                *

Mirando mi calavera
un nuevo Hamlet dirá:
he aquí un lindo fósil de una
careta de carnaval.

*

Enseña el Cristo: a tu prójimo
amarás como a ti mismo,
mas nunca olvides que es otro.

*

¿Dijiste media verdad?
Dirán que mientes dos veces
si dices la otra mitad.

Antonio Machado

Holding my skull one day
some new Hamlet will ask:
What is it we have here? A lovely
carnival mask.

*

Christ said to us love your neighbor as yourself,
but never forget that isn't who he is.

*

You told them half the truth? Be smart.
They will say you lied to them twice
If you tell them the other part.

Per Pasolini

Ormai se ti dico buongiorno ho paura dell'eco,
tu, disperato teatro, sontuosa rovina.

Eppure t'aveva lasciata, il mio verso, una spina.
Ma va' senza ritorno, perfetto e cieco.

Franco Fortini

For Pasolini

Desperate theatre, magnificent ruin. By now
if I say good morning I'm afraid of an echo. Never mind;

I leave you this verse, this thorn, anyhow.
Though you are gone for good now, perfect and blind.